# 39 Poems that Don't Stink!

## A Poetry Collection for Children

Kathleen A. Grover-Miller

# DEDICATION

For Mom. Thank you for sharing with me your love of language, for reading to me every night, and for making me look up in the dictionary every word that I ever asked you how to spell - even when that concept didn't make a lick of sense to me.
You are my hero.
xoxo


For Terri. You are the brightest star in the constellation of my life. Thank you for writing this poem for the book. I love it!
xoxo


## A LITTLE CAT

There once was a little cat, Kitty
Who knew she was so very pretty
She lied in the sun
Then went for a run
All the way in to the city

-T.M. Grover-Miller

# CONTENTS

Kathleen A. Grover-Miller

### In Memory of Patty

Your encouragement and support will carry me forward all the days
of my life. You were a wonderful cousin.
Rest in peace.
xoxo

# FORWARD

Poetry is one of the oldest art forms and yet many of us wrinkle our noses in displeasure at the mere mention of it. Maybe because the current trend is to view rhyming poems as contrived and old fashioned, while free verse, with its moody layers of complexity, is elevated. While one format seems out of date, the other leaves most of us scratching our heads as to what the author is talking about - too much work for those looking to relax with a few sacred minutes of recreational reading. Perhaps, poetry is extinguishing itself among the general population. And that's a shame because at its essence poetry is the voice of every soul. Without poetry we might never know the names Frost, Yeats, Platt, Cummings, Hughes, Poe, Tennyson, Browning, Anderson, Shakespeare, Dickenson, Homer or Angelou - artists who lifted words from ambiguity, one thoughtfully after the other, until – when given breath by the human voice, transformed into a spectacular dance of language. Poetry is emotive. It can sustain and heal, inspire and commiserate, record the past and shine hope at the future. It is what we are thinking, what we fear, what we value, what we honor. What begins as the deeply personal expression of the author becomes the deeply personal reflection of the reader.

The pieces contained in these pages are not something you're likely to hear at a poetry slam. In fact, most of these poems are traditional in structure and content as you would expect when the audience is children. They are silly, observational, reflective and thought provoking. The goal was to create a collection that would spark an interest in poetry at a young age, inspire an avenue for personal expression, serve as a soft place to land when there is a need to escape, and develop an appreciation for the wonder of words.

You'll notice that the beginning selections are geared toward the very young and then develop in appropriateness the deeper into the book you travel. I would be remiss if I did not add, that the tenor of my work is centered around the values of kindness, tolerance, empathy and inclusion. I want the kids who struggle because they feel different to know that I hear them and that they are not as alone as they think.

I structured this collection to resemble a poetry book that you yourself might have on your nightstand. There is a reason why I did not include illustrations. Children love to be read to. Poetry is personal. As you read aloud, your child will formulate his or her own images of what is taking place. Poetry aids literacy. Rhythm and beats in repetition help develop phonemic awareness. Stanza sequencing, combined with the tones and inflections of your voice build foundations for good readers and support memorization skills. Most of all, poetry is the expression of human spirit – the cadence of life and being. It is my hope that this little book will be the start of a lifelong interest in poetry for your child and that the moments you spend together sharing and revisiting these and other works will last a lifetime.

Kathleen A. Grover-Miller

# HOW I LOVE TO CLOMP IN BOOTS

How I love to clomp in boots -
*Gulumph! Galumph!* My burbling feet
Clumsy, thumping, smashing brutes,
Conquering sod and soil and peat.

All the dawn I trod and stride
From side to side and end to end,
Beyond the field, wet and wide
The silver trees and river bend.

But when I've a nagging hunch
That pulls and begs a swift retreat,
Signaling it's time for lunch
Off come the boots... Hello, bare feet!

## AVA SMALL THE MOUSE

"Are we to get a storm today?"
asked Ava Small the mouse,
"For I fear a sudden rain today
could wash away my house."

> "We need a thousand drops today,"
> replied her cousin, Pink -
> "The drought has left me parched today,
> and I could use a drink."

"I'll share this berry's juice today,"
a hopeful Ava said,
"If you will take me in today,
should floods wipe out my bed."

> "I'll gladly share my home today,"
> Pink answered with a sigh,
> "If you'll ignore the dust today;
> the dirt is desert dry."

"Without a pouring drench today,"
said worried neighbor, Lu -
"They'll be no flowers left today,
from which to gather dew."

> "The farmer's fields are scorched today,"
> observed Lu's sister Flo,
> "Without a stalk or seed today,
> I'm afraid we'll have to go!"

"I agree with Flo today,"
mocked difficult Maxine.
"These conditions are today,
the worst I've ever seen."

> "Yes, we'll say goodbye today,"
> her cousin Stink repined,
> "And find another place today,
> where the climate is more kind."

**"WAIT!!"** Ava Small threw up her arms.

Drip!
> Drip!!
> > Drip!!!

"Perhaps I'll try succinct today,
so please let me explain.
The sky has turned dark gray today
and it's begun to rain.

> So if you wouldn't mind today,
> I'd be one grateful mouse,
> If you would shelter me today,
> when squalls take out my house."

Ava left her nest today
within the gutter spout,
And moved into the barn today,
where other mice hang out.

Her drainpipe home she'll miss today,
its charm she can't deny,
But Ava Small feels grand today,
because her bed is dry.

## WHERE TODAY WILL LOTTIE LAY?

These days I'm hardly thinking,
No problems have I caught,
There is no senseless worry,
So worry I do not.

I do not need to read a book
Or climb a tangled tree,
To know the very right,
Exactly perfect, place for me.

It really is quite simple –
A train or car might do,
I balk at any cuckoo clock
Or smelly sock or shoe!

You might think a piano,
Or lovely winter caps,
Or jars for jams or pails for clams
Or blankets used for naps.

Goodness, not a trampoline,
A Ferris wheel or moat!
I'd have to say, "It's not okay!"
To choose under a goat.
Or on a bed of nails!
Or in a shell for snails!
Why, you could say a kangaroo!
And I would say, "A pouch might do!"

Or better yet, a treasure chest!
"Tres chic!" you ooze, "The gold...!"
*Sit upon a stack of coins?!*
Why that would be too cold!

One hundred zillion places!
Goodness! How to snooze?
Can I close my eyes at night
If I can't pick and choose?

Which answer is the right one?
I know how much you care –
Respectfully, I must decline
Your woolen underwear.

Atop the pillow of a troll?
On penguin's feet? Inside a bowl?
All great suggestions, this I say –
It's simply not my style, my way!

Please worry not my friend; I know –
The exactly perfect, place to go...
I am a hen and hens know best,
To lay their eggs inside a nest.

*I wrote this poem in tribute to Dr. Seuss and his whimsical verse. And yes... there is a real life Lottie. Her proper name is Charlotte and she shares her coop with her sisters, Emaline, Violet, Addie and Peaches.*

## SWEET MISS MAGEE

Our sweet Miss Magee, who's as sweet as can be,
Announced it was time to have snack -
So I ran past Louise, who was starting to sneeze,
And got to my cubby b'fore Jack.

I had barely unzipped my backpack when Kip,
Took a stumble, straight to a fall -
But he grabbed hold of Kyle, a bibliophile
Whose book about whales hit the wall.

Well that shocked Kareem, who started to scream,
Thinking it a thunderous clap -
And since he's scared of big storms (and bumblebee swarms)
He nearly collapsed in Jill's lap!

"Someone's fainted!" yelled Nell as loud as a bell,
"Miss Magee… should I get the nurse?"
But before her reply, Mia started to cry
And things went from rotten to worse.

"My lunchbox is missing!" she started hissing,
Then wailed, "I HAVE NOTHING TO EAT!!"
The calamity spread until Miss Magee said,
"Everyone, go back to your seat!"

## THE SONGBIRD

In the light at the first hint of morning
When the white-throated sparrow takes note,
A slow and clear whistle proclaiming
The promise of day fills his throat.

He sings for his love from the branches -
The boughs of the fir tree and then,
He joins in a bright sunny chorus
With the cardinal, the robin and wren.

## THERE ONCE WAS A SWEET KANGAROO

There once was a sweet kangaroo,
Who complained she had nothing to do.
So I brought her a goat
On whom she could dote,
And now she's a nanny-garoo!

## MARY BENNETT ATE A BEAN

Mary Bennett ate a bean,
Then she ate ten more.
She took them from a small display
Inside the grocery store.

*Free Samples While Supplies Last!*
Mary Bennett made a scene -
Gobbling up,
Every cup,
Of *Darla's Homemade Beans.*

"Delectable!" "Delicious!"
"Why, these beans are so divine!"
Not a single, scrumptious, savory bean
Did Mary leave behind.

*Twenty beans!*
*Forty beans!*
*Sixty beans!*
It's true!
Mary Bennett ate them all,
And licked her carriage, too!

With the final sample gone
Of *Darla's Homemade Beans,*
Mary Bennett walked away
In search of collard greens.

But then - within the produce aisle,
Mary heard a drum and flute –
A rumbling,
Grumbling base,
Followed by a tooty-toot!

*More samples!* She surmised with glee,
*Free salami at the deli?*
Or was the tooting coming from,
Mary Bennett's bean-filled belly?

## MOONRISE

When the sun softens into the sky turning it baby blue,
And the birds settle in among long branches,
The moon waits patiently for the nod to rise.

An hour passes,
    Then another

Before the chickens and ducks flock to the coop
And the frog finds a rock in the bog still warm from the day's
heat.

The dog comes in and the cat heads out;
Blossoms pull tight their lofty petals,
As fancy day bows to modest night.

And as they pass,
    One down -
        One up,

They loop their light in a timeless bob
Promising to meet again when the clock sings
And the cricket yawns under the shadow of the hardwood
log.

## MY RABBIT LOUIE

Nibble on a spray of oats,
Yawn and stretch as sunrays dote.
Bink in joy with shakes of straw,
Then wash your velvet ears with paw.

Nibble branch of apple sweet,
And when your tending care complete,
Bink again so I can see
How happy my sweet bunny be.

*When rabbits are feeling joyful they do their own version of a happy dance by jumping, twisting their bodies and kicking their feet in the air. This is called, binking.*

## EZRA CORNELIUS PAHDING

Ezra Cornelius Pahding
Woke up on the first day of spring.
He searched for the robin,
He searched for the doe,
But all he could see were white drifts of snow.
"UGH!" he exclaimed with frost on his head -
He slammed shut his window and went back to bed.

## BEWARE OF THE MONNAGOONIE

There's a creature that awakens
Whenever children cry,
It rises out of slumber
With a wretched, eerie sigh.

Upon the wind this thing detects
Each whimper, whine and wail,
With ears that snap like bubble wrap
And a telescoping tail.

Two small wings above its back
Three larger ones below,
Extra eyes with which to spy,
Emit a greenish glow.

They aid this stealth and agile fiend
In search of orbs that leak,
You'll never see or hear it slurp
The water on your cheek.

If you wrench or mewl or wrest
Or conduct a blubberfest,
The tiny thief will seek you out,
Your tears, his ardent quest.

So hitch your breath young royal -
Try not to be so looney,
It's the only way to keep at bay,
A thirsty MONNAGOONIE!

# FAST STEP EDDIE

Fast Step Eddie stepped in gum
Then tried to clean his shoes,
But sticky ick stuck to his thumb,
His hair and baby blues.

Frantically, he danced and spit
To rid himself of goo
But as he flicked and twisted it
Disgustingly, it grew!

Until the gum stretched o'er his nose
That wad of pre-chewed trouble –
Eddie sneezed and in the throws
Became a walking bubble!

## THERE ARE CHICKENS IN MY PANTRY

There are chickens in my pantry,
There are chickens on my bed.
There are chickens watching TV
From their perch atop my head.
There are chickens making French toast,
And chickens making soup,
Chickens everywhere I turn,
But none inside the coop!
They rest along my couch - these roosters, chicks and hens;
I used to count them one by one, but now I count by tens!
There are chickens in the bathroom,
Who use my purple comb,
They seem to have forgotten,
That this is not their home.
I am overrun with poultry!
Too many! I'll go broke!
Oh wait; this isn't what you think,
It's just a chicken joke.

*This poem was written as a nod to the famous Poet Laureate, Jack Prelutsky. While he dreamed of chickens, we raise them on our backyard farm. More than once a hen has made her way inside, which made me wonder... what would happen if chickens ran the house?*

# WHISTLEPIG

"Where are the beets?" My head spun around,
"And the peas I planted from seed?
Or the orange-red peppers I put in the ground
In the garden I came here to weed?"

"The cucumbers, too?!" I sighed in disgust,
"That crop was my personal best!
Without pickles to pickle the season's a bust.
Who is this insatiable pest?"

I lifted a prickly curlicue vine
Devoid of large canopy leaves;
I squinted and scowled at that garden of mine
And considered a full cast of thieves.

A squirrel? A songbird? (I heard one this morn),
A troubled skunk needing a meal?
Was it chickens out scratching that noticed the corn
And the lettuce and squash sealed the deal?

*What are you?* I wondered with hands on my hips;
I carefully scanned for a clue -
A rabbit would relish asparagus tips,
A chipmunk would eat it all, too.

My eyes fell to a hole in the wall
Of fieldstone that borders the plot,
The passage created enough room to haul
All the veggies this herbivore sought.

An overturned bucket I sat down upon
To consider just what I should do -
Most of the ripened plantings were gone
Leaving nothing this winter for stew.

I lamented the loss of astounding degree
When a rustling sound interfered;
Then out of the thickets, as bold as could be
The twig-snapping bandit appeared.

"Good day," said a groundhog in preoccupied flair;
"Good day," as he ambled on by.
"I can't stop to chat – I truly don't dare,"
Not once did he look in my eye.

His belly seemed stuffed - in a satisfied state
Which caused him to level more earth,
And remove yet another staging of slate
To allow for his increase in girth.

He started to munch on a small radish clump
Left behind from his last raid and pillage,
He had already taken tomatoes once plump
You'd think he was feeding a village!

"Hey! Hey! Hey!" I screamed waiving my arms
Demanding he cease and desist.
"Go ruin the harvest of some other farm!"
I pumped with a menacing fist.

He turned and retreated with greens in his mouth
Without whistling or grunting or force -
Into the scrub toward a slope facing south
To a hideaway burrow in course.

For three solid days I restacked those stones,
For three solid days he returned.
Until no vegetation was left but the groans
Of the ghostly garden he turned.

He wasn't deterred when I patched up the hole
Or each day when he hollowed once more,
Unwitting was he from whom that he stole
Except when I yelled, "This is war!"

It bothered him less than I felt it had me,
It bothered him perhaps not at all;
For he lumbered untroubled and blissfully free
While I reassembled the wall.

I prized his commitment to get the job done -
Perseverance in working the line,
And the only complaint that I have of his fun,
Is that the garden he ate through was mine.

*Groundhogs, (also known as woodchucks and whistlepigs) belong to a group of ground squirrels called marmots. They are interesting animals to learn about. One fact I learned the hard way, is that groundhogs are herbivores… as in, they look at gardens as their own personal salad bars!*

## I WAS FLOATING ALONG IN THE LAKE

I was floating along in the lake
When I heard someone scream, "THERE'S A SNAKE!"
So I swam for the beach
To be out of its reach
While my sister laughed, *"Oh, my mistake!"*

# WHY THERE SHOULD BE NO SCHOOL!

I have a case
That is clear to make,
A case that could change the rule
That forces every kid like me
To spend all week in school.

It's wrong and irresponsible,
It's wretched and it's cruel
To take away our time to play
And send us off to school.

The recess whistles never stop!
They screech inside my mind,
This makes it hard to concentrate
Throughout the daily grind.

> The dust of chalk,
> The lunch tray peas,
> The stone hard chairs,
> And those lines!
> The bells that blare,
> Hands up! Hands down!
> No talking, please!
> Pay the library fines!

The bus ride in, the bus ride home
Is bumpy and I fear,
Someday we'll hit a pothole and
The bus will disappear!

No laughing, joking, snorting too,
Lest time upon the stool
For having fun is just not done,
That's why I vote, NO SCHOOL!

I have to stop this writing soon
My teacher is nearby,
I like her very much you see,
And this might make her cry.

So hear me now,
I wish to learn.
A simpler way,
There must be.
I'm not a fool
To know that school is still the rule
Just not the place for me!

## TWO DOGS SLEEP

Two dogs sleep –
Head to tail, tail to head;
To each belongs a downy heap,
And yet in one they choose to bed.

## HE TOOK OUT A LIBRARY BOOK

He took out a library book,
To teach himself only to cook.
But when things went awry
And he sautéed his tie,
He created a new fashion look.

## RUNNING LATE

*You've lost your mind! Please, go away!*
I screamed inside my head,
To whomever it was that was shaking my shoulder
And looming over my bed.

"Get up!" "Get up!" Demanded the voice,
"You're already running late!"
But how can that be when the sky is still dark?
I pondered in silent debate.

"Get in the shower! I'll fix your lunch!"
Then my blanket was stripped to the sheets,
By precisely the person who insisted I rise
And drag myself out to the streets.

It's deep in the hours, midnight at least!
Who is this maniacal creep?
What kind of person wakes up another
Who's peacefully relishing sleep?

I covered my head with a pillow to hide,
I argued but no words came out.
If this is a nightmare, then what kind of creature
Is shaking my bones with its shout?

"I know you can hear me! Get up right now!
This is no time for fooling around!"
The voice was persistent, determined to hear
The sound of my feet hit the ground.

I mumbled and moaned in a fog of contempt
At the harasser who thought it alright,
To ransack my dreams and pry me from rest
By discourteously flipping the light.

I arose like a zombie, got dressed and descended
To the kitchen for some type of gruel,
As the rooster was crowing, the sky turned to pink
I remembered… the first day of school!

Reality hit me like a coconut hurled
By a monkey with a heck of an arm,
Summer was over and so was my sleep,
In its place - the human alarm!

The one who cajoled with laser-like briefings,
Tossed butter for hot toast to smother,
Who kissed me goodbye and then started to cry…
My beautiful, kindhearted mother.

# THE RED TAIL HAWK

The red tail hawk on current swoops,
How high its winsome dance today!
But "oh," sighs mouse beneath each loop,
"I recognize that dance of prey!"

## WHO AM I

Who am I?
I wish I knew -
I'm one of many and one of few.
Where I fit, I cannot find.
How to myself can I be true?

Those older say don't stress your mind,
What matters most is being kind -
The fog of feeling out of place,
Will someday soon be left behind.

It will get easier, this human space;
You'll know the heart behind the face,
And feel the gift of your own grace,
And feel the gift of your own grace.

# I SAW A FLOCK OF ANGELS FLY

I saw a flock of angels fly
They swept the sky,
My red hair, too –

I saw the leader
And caboose
Sixteen in all, above me flew.

I raced to follow wisps of white,
I raced to join their fancied flight,
Echoed swoosh propelled my feet,
I ran, I ran fast through the street.

I saw the shadows of their wings,
Create a twin on playground swings,
And trees,

Tops of roofs and steeples high,
They dipped, they turned and teased.

I wished so much to see them land,
To know if they could sit or stand,
And when they stilled, to ask them if
They knew the ones I loved and miss.

I watched a flock of angels fly,
They did not stop or wave goodbye,
Or slow,

Huff and puff my legs grew tired
And so,
I'll never know.

My friends say they weren't real at all,
That, splendid birds migrate in fall,
But I know what I watched go by,
I saw a flock of angels fly.

# IT'S WINTER'S CHILL I FEEL TONIGHT

It's winter's chill I feel tonight,
Though autumn holds the bragging right,
And summer's heat I still recall
It being just the first of fall.

But now with shortened lengths of day,
And hours less in fields to play,
I have to go to bed by eight
And like a grizzly, hibernate.

I slip between two freezing sheets,
And sure enough before two beats,
I start to shiver, teeth to spine
And protest loudly with a whine.

It doesn't take my thrashing form,
Too long to heat the linens warm,
And soon I'm drifting off to sleep
Burrowed beneath my blankets deep.

## OF DOGS AND CATS

Of dogs and cats, which reigns supreme?
Interesting question…
For equal seems their charming gleam
In gaining my attention.

Doting canine's love, it gushes!
In wagging tail and moon pie eyes;
Feline's coyness hides her blushes
And tender heart each purr implies.

Don't hold me to a solid oath
To choose the one I value best -
I'd have to say I love them both,
And equally my heart is blessed!

## FOUR TRAITS

Tolerant, Honorable, Ethical, Kind -
If you keep these four traits always in mind,
How lovely the echo your life song will ring,
And grateful the heart safe under your wing.

## TWO SQUIRRELS

Two squirrels chortle from a tree,
They warn of present danger.
I feel quite bad to know it's me,
They look upon as stranger.

So in a tender voice I speak,
In cadence slow and low,
I try to ease my own mystique
And beg them not to go.

But wary they in frozen glare
No squirrelly comment said,
Until the smallest of the pair
Hurls acorns at my head.

## LATE AFTERNOON

I watch you day, relinquish light
In tiny steps the change is slight
So not to frighten fragile leaves,
Which twist and shake in autumn's breeze.

I see your softened shadows grow -
They gently let the owl know
And in a whoosh from branch to bough,
He's perched above the field and plow.

I cannot stay to see this through,
For feed the stove and check the flu
And other chores are there to tend,
So goodnight day, my gentle friend.

## LIKE ICE

Like ice,
I am fragile.
I shatter when life booms,
I melt in the heat of discourse
Seeking refuge in deep layers of blue.
At times I am like the sparrow that turns
And shields against the blustery hail of a winter's storm
Waiting on the kindness of sunlight and the cheerfulness of
hope.
Sometimes the wait is long -
But always,
By chance or by fate,
A wind, warm and rousing
Lifts my delicateness
Above the cruel and noisy,
And I sing a most beautiful song.
And when this happens –
Like ice,
I am unbreakable.

FRIENDSHIP

I like your smile -
Sunny... youthful... lovely... inviting;
I could melt within its warmth
And be quite happy to stay.

## ZINNIA

Burst large your blooms of berry pink
And I of far off days will think
Of gardens bright with flowerheads
And patient hands that tend each bed.

Of lilting tunes hummed row by row
Where long and lovely green stems grow,
Of butterflies that dazzle air
Then tease a strand of light brown hair.

Of gentle wipes to dampened brow
And hazel eyes that teach me how,
In apron pockets clippings hide
While cuttings wait to go inside.

Burst large your blooms of berry pink
And I of far off days will think
Of gardens bright with flowerheads
And patient hands that tend each bed.

*I wrote this poem the day my mom told me how zinnias remind her of my grandmother. We miss her.*

# SHOES

A thousand miles I have walked
In shoes identical to yours,
I've put heal and toe to pavement,
And skirted drying tiled floors.

My shoes, like yours
Have traveled down that dusty country road,
They have kept the beat of drummers,
They have rushed and paused and strolled.

To work, to worship, to wander
Over rocks their leather bend
Home to where a loved one waits,
To the bus to meet a friend.

My shoes, like yours
Have traveled off to market for milk and bread,
They have shuffled, scuffed and sashayed
Until they rest beneath my bed.

My shoes, like yours
Have echoed inside an empty chamber hall,
But in crossing over thresholds,
Our shoes are not the same at all.
In crossing over thresholds,
Our shoes are not the same at all.

*Someone wise once said, treat all people you meet with an open heart because you won't always know the obstacles they face or the burdens they carry in silence.*

## WINTER SNOW

I love late December nights,
Shadows cast by amber lights
On icy blues and frosty whites
With balsam branches clumping.

Tender as an infant's sleep,
Snowflakes fall and pile deep,
No sound at all except the beat
My heart is softly thumping.

Flutter lashes fail but try
To keep ruddy cheekbones dry
While lungs exhale a peaceful sigh
And joyful soul is jumping.

## NANA

Every Sunday afternoon we drive into the city,
We pass by flowers in the park and alleys that are gritty.
We circle 'round the rotary and Mrs. Mangie's spouse,
Until we reach the tree-lined street
Where sits my Nana's house.

We spill into her parlor, in upholstered chairs some slouch,
But I sit next to Nana in the middle of the couch.
She straightens a small towel with unobservant care
The one she draped across the arm to mitigate its wear.

And as she catches up I note, with all the latest news,
My uncle joins us on the couch
To start his midday snooze.

It's later when these visits seem to take a comic twist,
Before we sit for dinner or a goodnight forehead kissed,
My nana's eyebrows shoot above her sparkly crystal frames,
My hand is squeezed – she's heard a noise,
Could I have heard the same?

There is no time to answer; she leaps up in a flash
And rushes to the window where she pulls the curtain back.
*"It's Mr. Walsh,"* she whispers, *"He's getting in his car.*
*He does the same thing every day and seems to travel far.*

*Sometimes he's gone for hours, without his kids or wife*
*There's something fishy going on. He leads a secret life!"*

I thought of asking Nana if perhaps he held a job
But before I could she offered,
That he may work for the mob.

I also learned that Mrs. Buck, who lives across the way,
Has packages delivered at the oddest times of day.
And Mr. Spry and Mrs. Jones and the man with greenish hair,
Have meetings every Thursday
On the porch of Margie Claire.

My dad pulls back the curtain from the other window pane
And seems to nod there certainly is more to be explained.
Then Mom shoots him a glance that says –
Please stay out of sight…
Staking out the neighbor's house
Is simply not polite.

But after weeks and years of watching Nana do her thing,
I have a different view on why she's always wondering.
My nana isn't nosy, in fact, she's rather sly,
And this is why I now believe
That Nana is a spy.

## GREEN SIDE UP IS HOW I GROW

Green side up is how I grow,
Thought the tiniest of shoots.
Goodness tills the toughest row
And kindness toughens up my roots.
I am good and I am kind
And being so inclined,
This hardened soil will not deter me,
That screeching crow will not intimidate me,
The blazing sun with its relentless heat will not wilt my tender
leaves
Or discourage
my
path
to
the
sky.
Green side up is how I grow
I grow for me.

## IT'S ALL RELATIVE

The next three poems are not mine. The first was written by my mom, and the two that follow, by my grandfather. Writing is part of my DNA. It's how my family expresses itself and at times, how we have supplemented our income - sometimes through prose, sometimes through lyrics and melodies, and sometimes through poetry. Both the works of my mother and grandfather have appeared in newspapers and periodicals over the years and a future project of mine is to assemble them all and republish them as a collection. I've always considered writing akin to the family business. I am thrilled to include these pieces because without their influence, I'd have all these thoughts floating around in my head and nowhere for them to land.

Oh, I almost forgot. The poem, *Beware of the Monnagoonie* on page 15 was inspired by my grandfather. He introduced every one of his grandchildren to the existence of this dreadful ghoul. We had a few close calls, but thankfully, with Grandpa on the lookout, not a single Monnagoonie ever got us!

One more note, because I know my mom is going to read this – thank you for being the best mother in the entire universe. (Even when you are a grownup, it's okay to tell your mom that she is awesome!)

xoxo

# WHEN GREAT GRANDMA WAS YOUNG

They loved to hear great grandma's tales
Of times when she was young,
Of childhood friends and games they'd play
Of all the songs they'd sung.

Great grandma's eyes were twinklin'
While talking of the fun
They had while playing hide and seek,
Jump roping in the sun.

She said they had no TV's then.
Can you imagine that?
A time without computers
For study or to chat.

She'd never seen an iPod,
A DVD or tape -
She listened to the radio
And thought the stories great.

Adventures you could think about
And pictures in your head,
Of pirates, cowboys and the like
As you went off to bed.

The girls would pass time playing dolls
While boys made carts of wood,
Or paper planes they tried to fly
Above the neighborhood.

Great Grandma made it seem so neat
To grow up as she did,
It doesn't seem so strange at all
To see her as a kid!

*-Kathleen A. McCarthy Grover*

## LADY OF LONG AGO

In a tiny shop where I chanced to stray
In the dust of years you were tucked away;
Your pretty face smiled tenderly
So I took you home with me.

Dear lady out of long ago
In your quaint old fashioned gown.
At night when I am dreaming
Come tiptoe softly down,
Your gentle grace
Your wistful face
Old memories recall,
By the firelight – forget tonight,
You're a picture on the wall.

*-Jeremiah F. McCarthy (1907-1977)*

## AFTER A RAIN SHOWER

Gray, somber clouds;
Black, angry clouds racing across the sky,
Patches of blue appearing through
The clean sweet smell of moist earth.
Parched fields drinking greedily,
Tall pines with dripping boughs,
A warm breeze stirring among the wet grasses,
Children with paper sailboats
Playing in puddles in the road.

*-Jeremiah F. McCarthy (1907-1977)*

## BE DONE WITH THE DAY

How do I call an end to this day
With so many thoughts left still to say?
I'll hold you in dreams and tenderly keep
Each meant-to-be verse alive while I sleep;
Then in the morning, I'll pick up my pen
And dance with you words, all over again.

Kathleen A. Grover-Miller

## ABOUT THE AUTHOR

Writer and humorist, Kathie Grover-Miller is a fan favorite of children and an ever increasing star among chickens and ducks. So much so, that Happy – the most industrious of her hens and author of *Happy's Journal – Daily Reflections of a Backyard Chicken*, encouraged her to publish this collection of poetry so she would stop wandering the yard reciting random verses when she should be dedicating her time to Happy's Journal – Part Deux. (Or something of a similar title so long as the name Happy is included. In bold letters. Maybe italics.)

Kathie lives in New Hampshire with her family. Along with being Happy's assistant, she is the author of *Moonlight Lemonade* and *The Quickie Book of Chicken Names*.

Made in the USA
Middletown, DE
26 December 2016